THE GOSPEL OF JOHN
BIBLE STUDY
BSBP SERIES
(Bible Studies for Busy People)

Margaret Weston is the author of
'How do I know I know God?'
a best seller in Christian Evangelism and the first book
in the 'How do I know?' series.
She is also the author of the BSBP series.
Full details can be found at
www.howdoiknowbooks.com

Margaret Weston is the author of 'How do I know I know God?' a best seller in Christian Evangelism and the first book in the 'How do I know?' series. She is also the author of the BSBP series. Full details can be found at www.howdoiknowbooks.com

All profit made by the author from this book is donated to Tearfund.

Tearfund is a Christian international aid and development agency working globally to end poverty and injustice, and to restore dignity and hope in some of the world's poorest communities.

Tearfund operates in more than fifty countries around the world. As well as being present in disaster situations and recovery through their response teams, they speak out on behalf of poor people on the national and international stage by petitioning governments, campaigning for justice and raising the profile of key poverty issues wherever they can. Find out more at www.tearfund.org

BIBLE STUDY (BSBP SERIES) FOR THE GOSPEL OF JOHN

CONTENTS

BSBP SERIES
(BIBLE STUDIES FOR BUSY PEOPLE)

The world is becoming increasingly busy and as Christians we are not immune from this. There always seems to be so much to do but so little time to do it! However, many of us love the Bible and would like to have more time to study it. So…………

The BSBP series has been prepared just for people like us – those who have a real desire to study the Bible but find they simply do not have enough time.

Do you want to study the Bible? Have you been put off by the length - and depth - of many of the books that are on offer? If your answer is 'yes' to these questions then the BSBP series is for you!

You will be taken step by step through your chosen book of the Bible - just 10 studies with 10 questions in each study. The brief supporting notes, will keep you focused on the job in hand. You will quickly and easily get a sound grasp of the subject matter - without having to use hours and hours of your valuable time!

These studies are ideal for both personal study and for stimulating thoughtful discussion within small groups.

The supporting notes roughly follow the order of the questions in each study. The best way to use the study is to first read the Bible section and prayerfully consider the questions. The notes can then be used either after each question to help stimulate thoughts or discussion, or when each study has been completed.

If you have any comments I would love to hear from you. You can find contact details on the following website: www.howdoiknowbooks.com

May God bless you as you study His Word and by so doing increase in your knowledge of Him.

The Gospel of John
Introduction

"Jesus did many other miraculous signs in the presence of his disciples, which are not recorded in this book. But these are written that you may believe that Jesus is the Christ, the Son of God, and that by believing you may have life in his name." John 20:30-31

The Gospel of John is not supposed to be a biography. John is writing because he wants us to be totally convinced that Jesus is the Son of God, God Himself come down to earth in human form. He wants us to understand that by believing in Him, our lives on earth will be changed and we will also find everlasting life. John wants us to know Jesus personally and find in Him water for this life, and also the water of everlasting life. And so this book is perhaps a theological argument, rather than a historical account of the life of Jesus.

John makes it clear in the very last verse of the book that he could not ever hope to cover the life of Jesus in one small book! There is so much to tell about all that Jesus did and said while He was on earth.

"Jesus did many other things as well. If every one of them were written down, I suppose that even the whole world would not have room for the books that would be written." John 21:25

From this we can understand the truth of the well known saying that this book is like a pool which is safe enough for a child to paddle in, but also like an ocean that is deep enough for an elephant – or indeed anything or anyone – to swim in. In one sense we can understand it with child-like faith, but in another we will never comprehend all that is in it, just as we can never fully comprehend God.

So we can see that the book is therefore suitable for new Christians. However, at the same time we will see that John may actually be writing not so much for beginners in the faith, but for those who know the basics of Christian truth and are willing to go further. We will need to take time to think about what is written and, as always, to ask for the guidance and help of the Holy Spirit, if we are to understand it correctly.

In the first chapter we are introduced to someone who is not named. There were two disciples who heard John the Baptist pointing to Jesus as the Lamb of God. Only one is named – Andrew – and the other one could well be John, who is thought to be the author of this book. However, he does not refer to himself by name but often speaks of the 'disciple who Jesus loved'. As we read this book let us remember that we too can have the same assurance. Each of us can enjoy this wonderful truth of being the woman/man/boy/girl that Jesus loves!

Many people throughout history have found that by reading and studying this wonderful book, the person of the Lord Jesus Christ becomes more real to them. It is my hope and prayer that this becomes true for each one of us. It is one of the greatest books of literature in the whole world - simple enough for children, but deep enough to confound the greatest intelligence.

We cannot possibly hope to cover this great book of John in 10 studies. Often you will find the questions and comments are only a snapshot of one particular part of the Gospel. This will hopefully cause you to want to know more and you will therefore read the entire book to make sure you do not miss anything out! I certainly encourage you to read those chapters and parts of chapters which are not covered in this study. May God bless you as you study this Gospel of John. My prayer is that you will keep asking the Holy Spirit for understanding, so that the result from this study is that you come to know Jesus better.

BIBLE STUDY
The Gospel of John

Study 1 – Chapter 1
The Word becomes flesh

Discuss/think about

Think about the last time you had a power cut and were plunged into darkness. How did you feel and what did you do? What effect does a candle or a torch have on the darkness around it? What effect does it have on you?

Read John chapter 1

1. The first words of this chapter are 'In the beginning'. Does this remind you of another place in the Bible which begins like this?

2. What/who is John talking about when he speaks about the 'Word'?

3. Sects such as the Mormons and the Jehovah's Witnesses do not believe that Jesus is God. How does this passage of Scripture help us to understand that Jesus is God Himself, come down to earth in human form?

4. Why is it so important to know that Jesus is God?

5. How does Jesus still shine as a light in the darkness today?

6. If we receive Jesus we become children of God. How does it make you feel when you remember that you are a child of God?

7. Read Isaiah 40:3. Why is John using these words to describe himself?

8. What does it mean to be 'baptized in the Holy Spirit'? (verse 33)

9. After meeting Jesus, what was the first thing Andrew did? Why do you think he did this? How can we be like Andrew?

10. List/discuss all the things this chapter has told us about Jesus.

Don't forget to pray – and read chapters 2 & 3 before the next study!

Ask the Holy Spirit to open your eyes so you understand who Jesus really is. Ask Him to give you the power to follow Him, like Andrew and Peter, and to shine as a light in this dark world.

John – Chapter 1
Study notes

As we begin to read the first few words of this chapter we are immediately reminded of Genesis chapter 1 – 'In the beginning'. So John wants to make it clear, before he says anything else, that Jesus – the Word – was there in the beginning with God. Jesus is God Himself, who came to earth in human form. John 1:14 explains that Jesus is 'the Word' – 'The Word became flesh and made his dwelling among us.'

The original word (for 'the word') in the Greek language is 'logos'. It is difficult to find an accurate English translation for this because of the scope of the word. Suffice to say here that it incorporates the idea of human reason together with divine or universal intelligence. Simply put, it shows God's desire to 'speak' with us and thus to form a relationship with us. The 'word became flesh' shows us God's desire and ability to link the human with the divine and provide the bridge which is necessary between the two, if we are to ever be able to have a relationship with Him.

It is very important to understand that Jesus is God because if we do not believe this then how can we be saved? If Jesus is not God – and merely a good man – then His death on the cross achieved nothing. We know that because of our sin we owe a huge debt to God that we are unable to pay. God is a righteous God and cannot overlook sin. It had to be Jesus that died as He was the only perfect man – one who did not have to die because of His own sin. Anselm of Canterbury explains why it had to be Jesus who paid the price. He says of the debt we owe to God, that 'no-one can pay except God and no-one ought to pay except man: it is necessary that a God-Man should pay it.'

Jesus still shines as a light in the darkness today because when we know Him as our Lord and Saviour He is able to transform our hearts and lives. Colossians 1:13 tells us that we have been 'rescued from the dominion of darkness and brought into the kingdom of the Son he loves…'

John always wants to point to Jesus and not to himself. He refused all the titles that others wanted to give him e.g. Elijah or one of the prophets. He refers to himself only as a voice pointing to Jesus. He wants us to connect with Isaiah 40 and understand the greatness of the One who is coming and to prepare the way for Him.

The phrase 'baptised in the Spirit' is somewhat controversial among Christians. Some believe that when we 'repent' i.e. turn away from sin and invite Jesus into our lives then we receive the Holy Spirit and in that sense are baptised in the Spirit. Others believe we must ask for the gift of the Holy Spirit in order to be baptised by Him. Another view is that this baptism is a special experience which comes after we become a Christian – a special overflowing or being filled with the Spirit on a specific occasion which leads to a dramatic change in our lives. The Bible does not really explain in detail what this phrase means so we should be careful not to be too dogmatic about any explanation. It is clear that we cannot live the Christian life without the power and help of the Holy Spirit. But we should also be clear that there are not two classes of Christians – one group who are baptised with the Spirit and one who are not. Different people may have different experiences in their Christian life but this should not be a source of pride. Each of us should always want to point to Jesus and not to ourselves, or our own experience.

We see a great example in Andrew of one who immediately wanted to point to Jesus. The first thing he did was to find his brother and tell him about Jesus. If we have a personal meeting with Jesus then we will find that we too want to tell others about Him.

This chapter has told us so much about Jesus. Some of these things are as follows. Jesus is the Word; He is God; He was there when the world was made; everything was made through Him; He is life; He is light; He became a man; He is full of grace and truth; He is the Lamb of God; He takes away the sin of the world; He is the Son of God; He is the King of Israel; He is the Son of Man...... and much more too! John covers many things in this chapter but he would certainly agree that there is so much more that can be said about Jesus. He is beyond our description and beyond our comprehension but is still willing to be our Saviour, Friend and Lord.

Study 2 - Chapter 3
Jesus teaches Nicodemus

Discuss/think about

What does it mean to be a 'Christian'? When did you first become a
Christian? Was this a dramatic moment when you met with Jesus or
did this happen over a period of time?

Read John chapter 3

1. Why do you think Nicodemus came to Jesus 'at night'?

2. What does it mean to be 'born again'? Why is this different
   from being 'religious' or being part of a religious group?
   (Nicodemus was a member of the Jewish ruling council.)

3. How do you know if you are born again?

4. Why is the Spirit likened to the wind in verse 8?

5. Can you be born again and not always aware of the presence
   of the Holy Spirit in your life?

6. Read Numbers 21:4-8. How do you understand this passage
   in relation to Jesus dying on the cross for us?

7. Why did Jesus speak about this passage in Numbers when He
   was speaking to Nicodemus about being born again?

8. What does John mean when he begins to speak about the
   'bride' and the 'bridegroom'?

9. John was not jealous when he was told that Jesus was
   baptising many people. He could have resented this. What
   can we learn from his attitude when we do God's work
   today?

10. Read verse 30. Do you feel like John? If not, why not?
    What can we do to make Jesus greater in our lives?

Don't forget to pray – and read chapter 4 before the next study!

Ask God to give you the conviction in your heart that you really are
'born again' and then ask Him to give you the power to live your
new life in a way that is pleasing to Him.

John Chapter 3
Study notes

Many expressions are used by different people to explain what happens to us when we come to know the Lord Jesus Christ. The Bible says, 'Believe in the Lord Jesus Christ and you will be saved….' Acts 16:31. Some people 'become a Christian' or 'meet with Jesus' or 'get saved' or 'find faith' or 'invite Jesus into their lives' and they usually mean that God has touched their heart and they have made a decision to believe in Jesus. Sometimes this happens suddenly and dramatically and some can pinpoint a specific moment or day when this change took place. With others this happens over a period of time and they are unable to remember a specific day or time when the change happened. The important thing however is not really when it happened, but the fact that it has. So today, can you and can I say that we have trust and faith in Jesus? And as we can see in this chapter, our eternal destiny hangs upon the answer to this question.

Nicodemus came to Jesus at night probably because he was afraid of someone seeing him. He was a member of the Jewish ruling council and would perhaps have been very aware of his position. Nevertheless he wanted to find out more and so he came to Jesus. We may be afraid or intrigued or have many other emotions, but if we come to Jesus then He will help us with every difficulty we may have.

There is some confusion about the term being 'born again'. Some Christians use this experience as if to differentiate themselves from other Christians. However, there are not different classes of Christians – some who are born again, and some who are not. To be born again means to be changed by God into a new person. 'Therefore if anyone is in Christ, he is a new creation; the old has gone, the new has come! All this is from God…….. 2 Corinthians 5:17. The person becomes different. He accepts the truth found in the Bible and wants to please God. As with being 'baptised with the Spirit' (discussed in the previous study) there may be a specific experience connected with being 'born again' but there may not. The important thing is to know if we are born again, not necessarily when it happened. We don't need our birth certificates to prove we are alive!

Being born again is obviously not the same thing as being 'Church of England' or 'Baptist' or 'Catholic'. It is easy to be part of a religious group and not be born again. Likewise we may be born again and not part of a religious group. However, if we are born again and want to please God, then we would usually want to find others who feel likewise, and work with them to build the kingdom of God on earth. Hence we would find ourselves as 'part of a religious group' or whatever term others may use to describe us!

If we have received the gift of the Holy Spirit and He lives in us, then we are born again. If however we are not sure about this, then we can ask God to give us the conviction in our hearts that we are born again. We must remember it is God's work and the reference to the Holy Spirit being like the wind reminds us that God can, and does, act however and wherever He pleases. We cannot limit God and He touches hearts and lives in different ways. We should not say, or think, that our personal experience is the 'right' one and that the experiences of others are better or worse. 'The wind blows wherever it pleases.'

We can grieve the Holy Spirit with the way we act and speak. Ephesians 4:30 says, 'And do not grieve the Holy Spirit of God with whom you were sealed for the day of redemption.' It follows therefore that even though we may have received the gift of the Holy Spirit and been born again, we can still behave as if He does not live within us. If we continue to do and say wrong things, and if we continue to sin, then it is unlikely we will be aware of His presence. He will retire into the background and we will lose the joy and peace we find when we allow Him to take control.

The serpent was lifted up as an answer to the sin of the Israelites. They had to look and live. Likewise, Jesus was lifted up on the cross for our sin and if we are to be saved then we too must 'look and live'. Jesus introduces this passage into the conversation because if we are to be born again we have to 'look and live'. We have to believe on the Lord Jesus and the work He accomplished on the cross. Coming to Jesus means coming into the light. Believing in Him means we have eternal life. Refusing to believe and rejecting Jesus means we remain in darkness with all its associated consequences.

In the Old Testament and some Jewish traditions, the Messiah was seen as the Bridegroom who was coming to make Israel His Bride. There would have been no doubt in the mind of his Jewish hearers that John was pointing to Jesus as the Messiah. He makes it clear that his job has been to point to the Messiah, not to compete with Him! We know too that in other Scriptures Jesus is referred to as the Bridegroom. As a result of the New Covenant we also know that the Bride is His Church i.e. that body of people which contains every person who has accepted Jesus irrespective of religious group, creed or colour.

We can learn from John's example not to be jealous of others who are working to honour the name of Jesus. They may not be part of our religious group, they may be different from us, but if they are honouring God and pointing to the Lord Jesus then we must thank God for that. Our concern should be to ensure that we are doing what God wants us to do and allowing the Holy Spirit to work in us and through us for His glory and honour.

Study 3 - Chapter 4
Jesus and the Samaritan Woman

Discuss/think about

Do you find it easy to talk to people about Jesus? How do you usually approach the subject? Do you find this easy or difficult? Discuss/think about why this might be.

Read John chapter 4

1. How did Jesus begin a conversation with this woman? What can we learn from this?

2. How would you describe the conversation? What was unusual about it?

3. Think about the method Jesus used to build up to very deep conversation about worship. What can we learn from this?

4. What does Jesus mean when He talks to the woman about drinking living water?

5. What does it mean to worship in 'spirit and truth'?

6. How does the woman try and avoid some of the truths in this conversation? How can we sometimes be like this?

7. This woman had a personal meeting with Jesus. What would/should be our reaction when we have a personal meeting with Jesus?

8. In verse 50 we read that the man believed Jesus and set off home. Why is it so important to simply believe what Jesus tells us?

9. Read John 20:29. We all like to see signs and miracles but this passage makes it clear that it is much greater to believe without signs and miracles. How do you feel about this?

10. What can we learn from this woman (in the first part of the chapter), and the royal official (in the last part of the chapter) which will help us in the way we live our lives today?

Don't forget to pray – and read chapters 5, 6, & 7 before the next study!

Remember to keep having personal meetings with Jesus. Ask the Holy Spirit to fill you with His love so that the effect in you is to reach out to others and tell them about Jesus.

John Chapter 4
Study notes

Jesus began to speak to this woman at a very ordinary level. He simply asked her for a drink. However, this was unusual because Jews did not usually speak with Samaritans. Furthermore, this woman was probably an outcast even amongst her own people because she was collecting water in the heat of the day. Most women would collect water in the cool of the day so they could stop and chat together. It seems this woman was trying to avoid others so she would have been surprised that Jesus spoke to her, even if it was just to ask for a drink.

We see that Jesus then begins to build a relationship with her. He moves the conversation onto a very important level and speaks to her about living water, worship and who He is. Wow! He manages to do this in a very short conversation. We can learn so much from this. We should be willing to reach out to those who are outcasts in society and build a relationship with them. We should also be willing to tell them about Jesus. There is limited benefit in helping someone in a material way if we do not also tell them about Jesus, and give them the opportunity of meeting the source of living water so they can have eternal life.

The conversation was in many ways a very ordinary conversation. However, it was very unusual in that it was between a Jew and a Samaritan; it led very quickly to a conversation about worship; the woman was not offended by Jesus referring to her many husbands; the woman went off immediately to tell others – even though she didn't fully understand what had happened; the woman became the first Samaritan evangelist as she told others about Jesus; and many more people came to know Jesus as a result of this conversation.

If we are willing to reach out to others on an ordinary level, then this can often become an opportunity to talk to them about Jesus.

The woman didn't really understand what Jesus was talking about (when he spoke about living water), but John speaks later in this gospel in chapter 7 about rivers of living water referring to the gift of the Holy Spirit. And note that the woman was encouraged to ask Jesus for this. 'If you had known you would have asked' – Jesus said – and so she asked for this precious gift. Likewise today we should be encouraged to ask God for the gift of the Holy Spirit, and keep asking to be filled with the Holy Spirit. Why do we need the power of the Holy Spirit? Because without Him we will achieve nothing for God. It is the Holy Spirit who will not only change our own lives but will give us the power we need to be able to transform the lives of others. We need power from on high if we are to bring others to the Lord Jesus Christ.

It is only with the help of the Holy Spirit that we can worship in the way that God wants us to worship – in spirit and in truth. There is a type of worshipper that God is seeking – one who worships in spirit and in truth. Spirit and truth perhaps correspond to the how and the whom of worship. These two words mean that real worship comes from the Spirit within and is based on truth – a true view of God. We must make sure we have a true view of God based on the Bible. If we don't know the Bible there is a danger we could be worshipping a God of our own imagination and not the one true God. Worship must have the heart and the head engaged. True worship comes from people who are deeply emotional and who love deep and sound doctrine. True worship affects every area of our lives. It also has a profound effect on those around us and changes lives.

The woman tries to change the subject when Jesus becomes very direct, just as we sometimes try to do this when He challenges us in different areas of our lives. However, if we allow Him to penetrate into every corner of our lives then the blessing will be immense. We will also find that as we meet with Him, our response will be to tell others about Him. It won't be because we feel it is our duty or obligation – although both these things are true – but it will be because we are so overwhelmed with His love and presence that we just have to tell others about Him!

The royal official believed what Jesus told him and set off home where he found his boy was living. It is a wonderful blessing to simply believe what Jesus tells us in the Bible. We can sometimes become so anxious to see signs and wonders that we miss the wonder of the Person who performs them. It is good to see and to hear about miracles but our faith should not depend on them but on the Word of God.

We can learn many things from the two main characters in this chapter who met Jesus. Perhaps the most important is to ensure we have a personal meeting with Jesus and to make sure we keep having personal meetings with Him. Then we will want to tell others about Him and thus the kingdom of God on earth will grow. Another important lesson to learn from this chapter is to believe the words of Jesus, rather then having to rely on signs and wonders.

Study 4 - Chapters 6 & 7
Jesus – the Bread of Life

Discuss/think about

We will see when we read some parts of John chapters 6 & 7 that there was a lot of discussion and disagreement about who Jesus was. Likewise today there are many different views and opinions about who Jesus was, who He is and even disagreement about who He will be. Who do you think Jesus is? Why do you think this and how did you come to this conclusion?

Read John chapter 6:25-70 and John chapter 7

1. What does Jesus mean in 6:35 and 6:51 when He says He is the bread of life?

2. How do we 'drink his blood' and 'eat his flesh' (verse 53)?

3. Why do some of His disciples find this teaching hard and leave Jesus as a result?

4. How do you feel about it?

5. Jesus' brothers accused Him of doing things in secret (v4) and thought He should 'show himself to the world'. Was this a true accusation? If not, why not? If the accusation was true, then why was Jesus not 'showing Himself to the world'?

6. Why do you think Jesus went up to the feast later on, rather than go with His brothers?

7. Identify the different reactions from various people to Jesus in these chapters. What reactions do you find today from people when they hear the name of Jesus?

8. Why did the Jews want to kill Jesus?

9. We read in 7:6 that Jesus said, 'the right time for me has not yet come'. Then we read in 7:30 that 'his time had not yet come'. Why had the 'time not yet come' for certain events, and what does this mean?

10. How did Jesus react to the opposition from a) His brothers, b) the crowd, and c) the religious leaders? What can we learn from this which may help us in our interaction with others?

Don't forget to pray – and read chapters 8 & 9 before the next study!

Ask God to open your eyes so that you can clearly see who Jesus is. Ask the Holy Spirit for courage to tell others about Jesus and for wisdom so that you know how to deal with their reactions.

John Chapters 6 & 7
Study notes

We hear a lot about different religions, different views and different opinions today. Atheists, Moslems, Agnostics, Buddhists and so on - but the key question that separates Christianity from other religions, and indeed anything else, is this:-'Who do you say that Jesus is?' People today have many different views about Jesus and in John's day it was no different. Others may tell us that their beliefs are similar to ours, but the question is – 'who do you say that Jesus is?' We have a personal relationship with a living person (if we do!) who is the Messiah, and no less than God Himself. This means that knowing Jesus is not just head knowledge, but heart knowledge. We/I know He is the Messiah, and He is also my Saviour, my Redeemer, my Friend and my Lord.

Just as we cannot live physically without bread or food, so we cannot live spiritually, and eternally, without Jesus. We feed on Him, i.e. eat His flesh and drink His blood, by taking in His words, digesting them spiritually and allowing them to affect our lives. Just as our natural bodies change as a result of food and drink so our spiritual lives are affected by the time we spend with Jesus, listening to Him and drinking in His words.

Some of His disciples found this conversation very difficult. Perhaps because they weren't prepared to take the time needed to understand it, and perhaps because they were not prepared for the cost of following Jesus. If we truly follow Him and eat His flesh and drink His blood, then it will have an impact on our lives. There will be a cost, e.g. mocking and maybe persecution, because we are different from others around us. We are different because we eat and drink different food!

When the people were discussing who Jesus was in Matthew 16:15-17, Peter says, 'You are the Messiah, the Son of the living God.' Jesus makes it clear that this is the right answer. 2 John 1:9 tells us that whoever continues in the teaching of Christ, has both the Father and the Son. Paul says in Galatians 1:8, that even if an angel from heaven says something different about Jesus, then we must not take any notice! So today, in the midst of different religions, different voices, different views and opinions, we can stay close to Jesus and say with Peter, 'You are the Messiah, the Son of the living God.'

We can only understand who Jesus is, if the Holy Spirit touches our hearts and reveals this to us. If we know Jesus we can tell others about Him, but then we must pray that the Holy Spirit will touch their hearts and lives.

The accusation from His brothers was true of Jesus because He did not want to make a public show. He always wanted the glory of God and not glory for Himself. If Jesus had followed the advice of his brothers to 'show yourself to the world' in *the way they thought he should,* there were two outcomes which could have resulted from this. Neither of them were the right ones in the plans and purposes of God. The first is that He could have been killed, and the second is that some people could have tried to make Him king. However, neither could happen *at that time* because that was not what God had planned. In accordance with God's plans, Jesus came to die on a cross, at a certain time, in a certain place, as a sacrifice for sin. And in God's plans Jesus will come again, at some future date, as a King. It is interesting to see however, that Jesus did indeed 'show himself to the world' when He came to the Feast – but most people did not recognise Him.

Jesus went up later to the Feast perhaps because He did not want a grand entry with everyone knowing He had arrived. It was not part of God's plan that He should join the crowd of pilgrims going up to the Feast, gathering followers and doing miracles as He went. If He had done this, the expectation would have risen that He was about to be declared the Messiah and become king. There was a tradition that the Messiah would come during the Feast of the Tabernacles, and it is interesting that Jesus did arrive during the feast and began to teach in the middle of it – the fourth day. Most of the crowd seemed to *miss this significant event* however because He did not arrive and act with great show and self promotion – *in the way they thought He should.* Do we sometimes miss out on what Jesus is doing, and where He is working, because He is not acting as *we* think He should?

There were different reactions to Jesus then, just as there are today, but there is only one right reaction. This is to acknowledge Him as the Messiah and know Him as our personal Saviour and Lord.

One of the reasons the Jews wanted to kill Jesus was because of their own self-righteousness. They relied on the law and they had a very high opinion of themselves as those who had studied the law, understood it and kept it. But Jesus made it clear that He knew their hearts and their thoughts and what they were really like inside. They were exposed and they hated it.

When Jesus says, 'my time has not yet come,' He is referring to the plans and purposes of God. He has come to fulfil all that had been prophesied in the Old Testament and to complete the work that God wanted Him to do. He would not be turned aside from this and He knew the right time and place for everything to happen. Thus He would not go to the Feast until the right time, and the Jews would not be able to kill Him until the right time according to God's plans.

Jesus responded to each challenge with a declaration of truth and with grace, i.e. an offer to believe in Him. We read in John 1:17, 'grace and truth came through Jesus Christ.' Some translations say, 'grace and truth *subsist* through Jesus Christ.' Both grace and truth are always seen in Jesus – thus He can condemn our sin (truth) but offer us the opportunity to be free from sin, if we believe in Him (grace). This wonderful grace is seen towards the end of the chapter when He says, 'if *anyone* is thirsty, let him come to me and drink. (italics mine)' The opportunity to come to Jesus is open to *everyone*.

So we can learn from this chapter to be more like Jesus when interacting with other people. We can demonstrate truth and grace. We need to tell others the truth about Jesus, invite them to meet Him for themselves, and pray that the Holy Spirit will touch their hearts so that they can understand who He really is.

Study 5 - Chapters 8 & 9
Natural and Spiritual Blindness

Discuss/think about

Close your eyes for a few moments and imagine what it would be like to be blind. Keep your eyes closed and discuss/think about how being blind would change your life. After your discussion open your eyes and describe how it feels to leave the darkness and come into the light.

Read John chapter 8:1-12; 8:42-47 and chapter 9

1. Why do you think Jesus did not immediately answer the Pharisees but bent down and wrote on the ground?

2. What does Jesus say to make it clear that He does not condemn the woman but He does want her to change?

3. How easy/difficult do you find it to condemn the sin without condemning the sinner – a) in your own life and b) in the lives of others?

4. Why does Jesus stress again in 8:12 that He is the light?

5. Jesus uses some very strong language in 8:42-47. Why is it necessary for Him to do this?

6. Why did the disciples think that either the blind man or his parents must have sinned?

7. Why do you think the man had to obey the instruction of Jesus to go and wash before he was healed?

8. Even though the Pharisees saw this miracle, they still did not believe. Why do you think this was?

9. Why did Jesus seek out the man again (9:35) after he had been healed?

10. How can we be spiritually blind? What is the cure for this?

Don't forget to pray – and read chapters 10, 11, 12 and 13 before the next study!

Ask the Lord Jesus to heal you of any spiritual blindness that you may have regarding who He is. Ask Him to give you a real conviction in your heart that He is the light of the world and that without Him you will be lost in the darkness.

John Chapters 8 & 9
Study notes

We are not told why Jesus wrote on the ground or what He wrote. There are various views about this. He may have written what He later spoke, so that the 'sentence' was written down as well as pronounced. Then there could be no doubt about it. He may have written down some of the sins of the accusers. In ancient times teachers would sometimes write or draw in the dust to explain things. He may have been making a point about how quick they were to condemn this woman, or giving them time to consider their position. But when the answer came it would have been devastating to those who heard. They considered they were so righteous, but when the light comes into our lives it exposes every dark corner.

This story of the woman caught in adultery makes it very clear that Jesus – the Light of the world – will expose our sin. We cannot hide from Him. However, this is only because He wants to forgive us, and He wants us to change. We know that sin always damages someone – either ourselves or someone else, and often both. Jesus therefore is willing to forgive, but He also expects us to turn our back on the sin. Jesus does not say that the law is wrong, but He is condemning the attitude of the Pharisees to it. It would be easy to use this passage as an excuse to sin, knowing that we can be forgiven. But the last words of Jesus to the woman are, 'Go now and leave your life of sin.'

Jesus stresses again that He is the light. He has exposed the darkness in the lives of the woman's accusers and He then goes on to make it clear who He really is. However, because the Pharisees were spiritually blind, and in darkness, they were unable to recognise the light. We can sometimes turn away from Jesus – the light of the world – because we are unwilling for the dark corners of our lives to be exposed.

Jesus then goes on to use some very strong language against the Pharisees. He wants them to listen and to change. He is giving them further opportunity to believe in Him and to move from the darkness into light. He is distressed at their hard hearts and is making clear to them that they are on a very dangerous path. There is a choice for each of us – light or darkness – and there is no middle road.

The disciples thought that the man was blind because of some specific sin committed by his parents, or by the man himself. They did not understand that we are affected by the fact that sin is in the world, and when bad things happen it is not necessarily because we ourselves have sinned. Of course we know that there is always a consequence from sin, and we often have to accept the consequence of our own actions. But we also know from the book of Job that bad things happen to good people. Job's friends believed that he was suffering because he had sinned. God makes it clear however, that Job was a righteous man and what was happening to him was not a direct result of Job having sinned.

We are not told why Jesus asked the man to go and wash before he was healed. It may have been that he wanted him to be obedient and believe what Jesus was saying, before the actual healing. We often have to act in faith and obedience before Jesus acts.

It is clear that miracles, in themselves, do not cause people to believe. It is only if God touches the heart that we are able to believe. We should therefore take care not to place too much emphasis on miracles, lest the miracle becomes the attraction rather than the One who has performed it! The Pharisees rejected Jesus and were therefore unable to believe, even though they saw a great miracle.

Jesus found the man again after he had been rejected by the Pharisees, perhaps because He wanted to reveal who He really was. What a wonderful compensation for this man who had been rejected by others. Jesus found him and told him who He was. It is often at times when we are rejected by others, or are in difficult circumstances, that we receive a special touch from Jesus and a special awareness of His presence.

Even when we are Christians we can become spiritually blind. We fail to see where God is working and what He is doing, or we use His word to justify ourselves or our actions. The only cure for spiritual blindness is to ask God to heal us. We need to ask Jesus to shine His light into every area of our lives. We need to come to Him and ask for the power of the Holy Spirit each day so that we do not become spiritually blind.

Study 6 - Chapter 13
Jesus is betrayed

Discuss/think about

Do you find it easier to serve others or to let them serve you? Have you ever had the opportunity to do something kind for someone who you know really dislikes you? How did you feel about this?

Read John chapter 12:29-36 and chapter 13

1. What does Jesus mean when He speaks about the grain of wheat dying and producing many seeds?

2. The events in this chapter occurred just before the Passover Feast. What was the Passover and why was it significant that Jesus was teaching the disciples in this way just before the Passover?

3. Why do you think Jesus washed the feet of the disciples?

4. Why did He include Judas, even though He knew Judas would betray Him?

5. Why did Peter want his whole body washed? And why did Jesus say Peter only needed his feet washed? What do you think this means for us today?

6. Jesus says in verse 15 that He has set us an example and in verse 16 that a servant is not greater than his master. How do you interpret this in the way you live your life today?

7. In verse 20 one of the disciples is referred to as the 'disciple whom Jesus loved.' We know Jesus loved all the disciples, so who do you think this refers to and why is this disciple described like this?

8. Why do you think Jesus gave the bread to Judas and didn't just name him as the betrayer?

9. How easy/difficult do you find it to keep the commandment Jesus gives in chapter 13:34? Is it possible to keep this commandment all the time?

10. What can we learn from Peter in this chapter?

Don't forget to pray – and read chapters 14-16 before the next study!

Ask God to help you follow the example of Jesus in the way you serve others. Ask the Holy Spirit to give you a real conviction in your heart that you are the 'man/woman who Jesus loves.' Ask Him to empower you with His love so that you can follow Jesus and be a light in the darkness for others.

John – Chapter 13
Study notes

When Jesus speaks about the grain of wheat dying and producing many seeds He is, of course, referring to His own death on the cross. As a result of that death many people are able to have eternal life - 'bringing many sons to glory' Hebrews 2:10.

When John mentions a Jewish festival he wants us to know that Jesus is applying its meaning to Himself. Jesus is the Passover Lamb (1:29, 36). He spoke at Passover of the Temple being destroyed and rebuilt, meaning His body (2:19-21). He fed the crowds at Passover time and spoke of them feeding on His body and blood in chapter 6. Now He is back at Jerusalem for a final Passover explaining what the meal was all about and pointing to the events of the following day.

When Jesus took off His outer garment to wash the feet of the disciples, it would have probably left Him dressed in only a tunic, in the same way as a slave would have been dressed to serve a meal. This was obviously not what anyone would expect a master to do. According to Jewish custom not even a Jewish slave would be expected to do this, only a gentile slave. So, Jesus was teaching his disciples a lesson in humility and service. He wanted them – and us – to understand what it really means to be a servant.

We see the great love of Jesus demonstrated here in that He washed the feet of Judas, even though He knew that Judas would betray Him. We read in chapter 13 verse 2 that the devil had already put the thought into the heart of Judas, to betray Jesus. So we have Jesus showing love to the uttermost (verse 1) followed immediately by the great betrayal (verse 2).

Peter did not understand what Jesus was doing and for him it was unthinkable that Jesus would act in this way. There were strict cultural status boundaries in that day and Jesus was completely violating these, in Peter's view. Then when Peter realised that Jesus really did want to wash his feet, he went to the other extreme and wanted his whole body washed. It seems that Peter did not understand what Jesus was doing, or why he was doing this. Today we have an advantage because we can read the whole of the Gospel of John and know what comes next! We can understand that Jesus is applying this washing in a spiritual sense. When we know Jesus as our Saviour and accept all He has done for us on the cross, we are washed clean from our sin. Then we have to ensure day by day that we keep clean. This could mean that we confess our sin daily and become clean again. Just as we pick up dirt and dust on our feet as we walk through life, so we also pick up dirt and dust spiritually through sin, and we have to confess our sin and become clean again. 1 John 1:9.

Most scholars believe that when we read about 'the disciple whom Jesus loved' this is referring to John himself who most believe wrote this book. It is a lovely touch from John, showing his conviction that Jesus loved *him.* It can also be the same for us when we realise not just that God loves 'the world' John 3:16, but that Jesus actually loves *me* personally.

Dipping the bread and giving it to Judas may well have been a gesture of honour in that day, and many believe this could have been a final appeal to Judas to turn back from his betrayal. It could be a sign that Jesus still loves those who reject Him today. The disciples did not understand what was happening which was quite understandable, since Jesus continued to treat Judas as a friend even though He knew Judas would betray Him.

We will find it impossible to keep this new commandment in our own strength. The standard seems far too high – to love like Jesus. This commandment goes way beyond our human inclinations and is only possible if we are empowered by the Holy Spirit. God's love goes far beyond the desire to be loved back in return. Christ loved Judas in spite of his betrayal. God's love is perfect and has been demonstrated perfectly at the cross. It is impossible to love like this without God's power within us. We are called first to love and serve God, and then to love one another. It is to a sacrificial love that we are called, which is demonstrated perfectly in Jesus.

We can learn from Peter in this chapter, as someone just like some of us - enthusiastic but flawed, but nevertheless having a sincere love for Jesus. And it was on this 'rock' that Jesus has built His church. In Peter we find great encouragement. He was a man who made many mistakes but still Jesus says to him – 'And I tell you that you are Peter, and on this rock I will build my church, and the gates of Hades will not overcome it.' Matthew 16:18.

Study 7 – Chapters 14, 15 & 16
Jesus speaks with His disciples

Discuss/think about

Do you consider yourself to be a disciple of Jesus? What are the characteristics of a disciple? Do you think of Jesus as your 'best friend'? Discuss or think about why or why not.

Read John chapters 14, 15 & 16
(Although this is a lot to read at one time these are very important chapters. They contain words from Jesus Himself and we can learn so much here. Therefore, if you are unable to read all three chapters completely during this study then make sure you read each chapter at some other time and ask God to speak to you through them.)

1. What does Jesus mean when He says, 'I am the way and the truth and the life'?

2. What effect will it have on our lives if we truly believe this?

3. What does Jesus mean when He says, 'You may ask me for anything in my name, and I will do it'? (See 14:13-14)

4. How does the 'Counsellor', the Holy Spirit, help us?

5. What is Jesus teaching His disciples by using the illustration of the vine and the branches in chapter 15?

6. How do you feel about the 'pruning' that must take place so that we bear more fruit? Why is this necessary?

7. How easy/difficult is it to follow the Lord's command to 'love each other as I have loved you' (15:12)? What is the ultimate test of love that one person can demonstrate for his or her friend?

8. How do you feel about being a 'friend' of Jesus?

9. How do you think Jesus felt about leaving His disciples (chapter 16) and knowing that they would 'weep and mourn'? How do you think He feels about us when we are going through troubles and trials?

10. Chapter 16:33 ends by telling us we can have peace, but also that we will have trouble. How can we reconcile these two statements?

Don't forget to pray – and read chapters 17 & 18 before the next study!

Ask the Holy Spirit to help you experience the presence of Jesus every day, and especially when you pass through troubled times, so that you can really experience His peace.

John Chapters 14-16
Study notes

There are many characteristics of disciples but the primary characteristic would be love – love for God and love for others. Jesus clearly teaches that we should put God first in everything, and then 'love your neighbour as yourself'.

Some of the other characteristics of a disciple would be as follows:- being ready to follow where the Holy Spirit leads, and to submit to Him in everything; knowing the Word of God – or wanting to know the Word of God – and trying to apply it to all areas of life; being bold in telling others about Jesus, because our own lives have been so impacted by God; praying about everything; having peace in our hearts; representing Christ to the world around; living lives which are morally pure and recognising that our entire life should represent an act of worship; and many more qualities not mentioned here. Of course we often fail in many of these areas but this does not disqualify us from being disciples. But if we really desire to follow Christ, and want all these characteristics, then we can ask the Holy Spirit to work in us and through us so that we bear fruit in these areas.

'I am the way and the truth and the life' is one of the seven 'I am' statements used by Jesus. 'I am' in the Greek is a very strong and emphatic way of referring to oneself. It really means – I, me and only me – or something similar to that. We know that God told Moses that His name was 'I am'. So Jesus is making clear that it is *only* He who is the way, the truth and the life. He is the *only* way to the Father. He is the *only* way that makes any sense in this life. He is the complete and absolute truth. If we want to know the truth we look at Him and listen to Him. And He is the *only* way to a full, satisfied and complete life on this earth – as well as the source of everlasting life.

If we truly believe this then it will have a dramatic effect on our lives, and we would become true disciples with all the characteristics listed above, and many more as well. We would bear 'good fruit' as described in Galatians 5:22.

To ask for anything in the name of Jesus does not mean simply tagging His name on the end of our requests! If we ask for something in His name, then it would obviously need to be something that has His approval. This is similar to the statement in 1 John 5:14-15 where John speaks about asking God for anything 'according to His will'. God will only give us good things. Other Scriptures make it clear that we can, and should, ask for anything. But we ask in faith, knowing that God is good and that He will always do the very best for us, even if it sometimes does not appear that way to us.

The Holy Spirit helps us in so many ways. He is a Counsellor and therefore He is able to advise us, listen to us, comfort us and change us. We also need His help when we pray, so we know *how* to pray. He spreads God's love in our hearts and gives us love for others. Without the help of the Holy Spirit we can never please God.

The use of the vine and branches as an illustration in chapter 15 teaches us what it means to ask for things in the name of Jesus. The main job for the branch is simply to remain connected to the vine. If it does this, then everything else happens as it should do. It will grow and bear good fruit. So our primary objective should always be to keep close to Jesus. If we do this, we will learn how to live our lives here in the best way, how to ask Him for all that we desire – in His name, how to cope in difficult times, and so much more. If a branch tries to leave the vine and go off and do its own thing, it will quickly lead to death and disaster.

Just as pruning must take place with vines and other trees and plants, so pruning must take place in our lives if we are to bear good fruit. There is much in our lives which must be changed, if we are to become like Jesus. God's purpose in our lives is to make us more like Jesus. Pruning is sometimes quite drastic and often painful, but as we read in the book of Hebrews (12:11), and elsewhere, afterwards we will rejoice that it has taken place.

Jesus demonstrated the ultimate test of love in that He was willing to lay down His life for each one of us. We cannot love one another in a right way without the help of the Holy Spirit. If we feel we do not love someone as we should, we can ask the Holy Spirit to change the way we feel, and He will do this.

It is a wonderful privilege to be a friend of Jesus. As we spend time with Him and get to know Him better, He will share with us some of the things He is doing in our lives and the lives of others. We can only get to know Him better by spending time with Him.

No doubt Jesus was very sad about the effect He knew it would have on His disciples when He left them. He would have been very sympathetic and compassionate about this, just as He is when we go through troubles and trials. However, He knew that this had to happen for the ultimate blessing of the disciples. He also knows that sometimes we have to go through troubles and trials for our own ultimate blessing, but He is always there beside us to help us through.

If we are true disciples then we will have trouble in this world. Jesus tells us this. He also says that a servant is not greater than His master, and to take up our cross and follow Him. So we cannot expect life to always be easy although there are, of course, often times of great blessing or 'green pastures' (Psalm 23). However, we know that Jesus has won the victory over death, so whatever we go through here on earth we have the assurance of ultimate victory and everlasting life with Him. We can also know peace in our hearts by having the experience of His presence, while we are going through difficult times.

Study 8 – Chapter 18
Jesus is arrested

Discuss/think about

Have you ever been hurt by someone you thought was your friend? How did this make you feel. Have you ever been ashamed of being a Christian, and not been able to tell people about Jesus when you know you should have done so? How did you feel about this?

Read John chapter 18

1. How would you have felt if you had been with Jesus in the garden when Judas arrived?

2. How can we see in this chapter that Jesus is still in control, even though these terrible things are happening to Him?

3. Why did Peter act as he did, first by using his sword on Malchus and then denying Jesus? How do you think you would have reacted in similar circumstances?

4. When do you find it hardest to tell people that you know Jesus?

5. How do you think Jesus felt about Peter's denial? How does He feel about us when we don't want to identify ourselves with Him?

6. List all the characteristics of Jesus that shine out in this chapter.

7. Why is Pilate so interested in knowing whether Jesus is a king or not?

8. Pilate is obviously very cynical about truth. What happens if we try to persuade ourselves, as some do, that truth does not exist and it is all a matter of opinion?

9. Why did the crowd choose Barabbas rather than Jesus?

10. What would help us to be more faithful to Jesus even in difficult circumstances?

Don't forget to pray – and read chapters 19 & 20 before the next study!

Ask the Father to help you to never forget all that Jesus went through because of His love for you. Ask Him to give you the strength and courage you need to be a good witness for Him. And ask that you will appreciate the love of Jesus so much that you will not be afraid to tell people about Him.

John – Chapter 18
Study notes

Jesus knew what was going to happen. He says, 'Shall I not drink the cup the Father has given me?' He asks the soldiers questions, He doesn't try and hide or run away. He helps Peter deal with the situation. But above all, He uses the 'I am' statement once again. Of course in the context of the discussion with the soldiers it could be viewed as an obvious statement, but it seems that they realised the power and authority of this person who was, and is, 'I am'. This must surely be the reason the soldiers fell to the ground. They knew the significance of the name of God – 'I am'. I am... the bread of life, the light of the world, the resurrection and the life, the way and the truth and the life. God Himself, come down in human form.

Peter seems to have an impulsive nature, but he loves Jesus. He wants to protect Jesus and thinks only of how to do this in human terms. He then succumbs to the pressure from those around him and goes on to deny Jesus. Jesus was, no doubt, affected by Peter's denial. It must have made Him very sad, just as it grieves Him when we deny Him or act in a way which is unworthy of Him. Nevertheless it is a great encouragement to us that Peter's failures are recorded. We can see in him characteristics that we find in ourselves. We may have great love for Jesus but still we fail. Nevertheless the love of Jesus for Peter, and for each one of us, is unchanged – even when we fail so badly and let Him down. As we continue through this Gospel of John we will be able to see the wonderful interaction later between Jesus and Peter.

There are many wonderful characteristics of Jesus which shine out in this chapter. Some of these are as follows:- His great love; His power; His wisdom; His submission to the will of His Father; His courage; His strength; and so much more than we can list here.

Pilate understood about kings, and politics, and how kings came to power. He seemed curious about why Jesus thought He was a king, because in Pilate's view Jesus was nothing like a king. For Pilate a king was someone who was a terrorist or revolutionary, trying to oust the Romans from Palestine. Jesus did not act like a king or look like a king. So for Pilate it must have seemed to be a very strange rumour or thought that he had in his mind about Jesus. The same problem arises in minds today. Jesus may not act today in the way we think He should, or in the way a king should, in our minds. This was the root of the problem for many when Jesus came to earth. They were looking for the Messiah, a King who would arrive with much pomp and glory and overcome all opposition. God's ways are not our ways! There will be a day when Jesus will come with glory and honour, but for now His kingdom is hidden from the eyes of those who will not accept Him as their Lord and Saviour.

Pilate seemed to be a very good politician. We know that many politicians feel like Pilate – what is truth? Truth today is viewed by many as non-existent. It is simply how I feel, or my opinion, or my view. Once we decide there is no absolute truth, then we give ourselves an excuse to behave in any way we wish. If it feels good it must be okay. Absolute truth is rejected, just as Pilate rejected the concept. Without Jesus we will never understand truth – because, as we saw in the previous study, He is the way *and the truth* and the life.

The world chose Barabbas, an evil-doer, and the world has suffered the consequences of this ever since. There were many reasons that Barabbas was chosen. For some it was no doubt political, for some it was fear, for some it was jealousy. If Jesus had come in today's world, the choice would have been no different. Of course we know that none of this took God by surprise, and He was working out His great plan of redemption for mankind. But this does not in any way excuse those who crucified Jesus. They made the decision from their own freewill. We can never excuse our sin, because we always have a choice. If we thought about the effects of sin and death in the world, it would make us more careful about what we do, and more grateful for all that Jesus has done for us. There are always consequences from sin, even though God may choose to limit these. And, of course, there is always forgiveness if we turn away from the sin and turn to God in repentance.

We need the help of the Holy Spirit to remain faithful to Jesus. He reminds us of the great love that the Lord has for each one of us. We would perhaps be more faithful if we remembered how much unfaithfulness affects God. We are upset and sad if our friends betray us or let us down, and throughout the Bible we see a God who has great emotion. Jesus displayed great emotion in the Gospels and He is grieved when we deny Him or turn away from Him today. We should pray often that the Holy Spirit will help us to always be true to Jesus, even if we are in very difficult circumstances.

Study 9 – Chapters 19 & 20
Jesus' death and burial

Discuss/think about

Have you ever been tempted to compromise and not act in a way you think is right because of pressure from those around you? Why did you act as you did and how did you feel about this?

Read John chapter 19 and chapter 20:1-9

1. Why was Pilate so interested in whether Jesus really was a king?

2. What kind of person was Pilate?

3. Who was responsible for the death of Jesus?

4. If you had to describe Jesus' kingdom to Pilate, what would you say? What kind of King was Jesus and why was this difficult for people to understand?

5. Read Psalm 22:1; 22:6-8 and 22:18. How do these verses relate to what is happening in this chapter, and how could they have been written so many years before Jesus was crucified?

6. How many people were brave enough to identify with Jesus when He was on the cross? Who were they? Where would you have stood?

7. What did Jesus say when He was actually on the cross and what do these statements teach us about His character and the work He came to do?

8. Why did the soldiers pierce Jesus with a spear, rather than break His legs as they did with the other two men who were crucified with Him?

9. How many witnesses are there in chapter 19 that Jesus was actually dead? And how many witnesses are there in 20:1-9 that the tomb was empty?

10. What is the significance of the grave clothes being arranged in a neat and tidy way?

Don't forget to pray – and read chapter 21 before the next study!

Remember to thank the Lord Jesus for all that He suffered for you and for me. Take time to re-read chapter 19 in His presence and remember that He went through all this because of His love for *you*.

John – Chapters 19 & 20
Study notes

We know from history books that Pilate was an ambitious and political man. He came to Judea and his official title was procurator of Judea. He came, hoping that he would soon be promoted – hopefully elsewhere. But things did not seem to go well for him in Judea. He made some political blunders and found himself almost at the mercy of the Jews, who knew that with enough pressure from them, he would do as they asked. It is in this situation he finds himself when Jesus is on trial.

Pilate is a man who is trapped. He has to act because of pressure from the Jews but at the same time he is afraid (19:8). Is Jesus really a king? And what is more, the Jews now tell him that Jesus claims to be the Son of God. What a predicament. It is clear that Jesus has been delivered for trial because of hate and envy, and not because He has done anything wrong. What is Pilate to do? He takes the easy way out and succumbs to pressure. His career meant more to him than to do what was clearly right and release Jesus.

We could say Pilate was responsible for the death of Jesus because of his weakness and ambition. We could blame the Jews or the Romans. We could blame the crowd. But the truth is that everyone of them played a part in the death of Jesus – just as every one of us who has sinned, have also played a part. We may not have been there, but our sin nailed Jesus to the cross in such a way that the only way He could have been freed, is if God's plan of redemption for mankind was given up. It was His love for each one of us that kept Him on the cross, and made Him willing to endure all that we read about in these chapters.

Jesus makes it clear that His kingdom does not come from this world. The world, as we see again and again in this Gospel, represents the source of evil and rebellion against God. So His kingdom is not *from* this world, but it is *for* this world. What love and grace! It is a kingdom which is so different from the kingdom/s of the world that we cannot understand it unless we know the King. If Jesus' kingdom had been from this world, then His followers would have fought for Him to subdue those around them. This was Pilate's concept of kings and kingdoms. Instead, the kingdom of which Jesus spoke was based on truth – the truth displayed in the person of Jesus. A kingdom in which one man dies, and the others go free. A kingdom based on truth and love and righteousness. A kingdom far removed from anything Pilate had ever known.

Psalm 22 is a prophetic Psalm and would probably have been one of the most popular prophecies for the early Christians. It was written long before Jesus came to earth, and yet it depicts the suffering and anguish He went through, as well as several of the events that happened around the cross. It would have been – and still is – a great comfort to Christians as to the truth of the Bible, and the fact that God was still in control even in the midst of the awful suffering of the Son of God.

There were not many who were brave enough to stand by Jesus when He was on the cross. John tells us about five of them:- Mary, the mother of Jesus; Salome (His aunt) who was the mother of John (who wrote this gospel); Mary the wife of Clopas; Mary Magdelene and John himself.

Jesus made seven statements or utterances when on the cross and John records three of these in these chapters. Jesus spoke to John about taking care of His mother, showing real love and concern even when suffering such agony. He said He was thirsty which not only tells us more about His suffering on the cross, but also strangely fulfils another prophecy in Psalm 69:21. Then He said those wonderful words, 'it is finished' showing that His work on earth and on the cross had been completed. The word in Greek means that a debt has been paid in full. He had completed what the Father wanted Him to do, and accomplished the wonderful work of redemption for mankind. What a Saviour!

Once again we see the fulfilment of prophecy as the soldiers did not break the legs of Jesus as they did with the others who were crucified with Him. The soldiers were confident that Jesus had died and therefore saw no need to break His legs. We know that no bone of the Passover lamb was to be broken. Jesus was the true Passover Lamb.

The significance of the blood is very important. All through the Old Testament we see that the blood being shed is a very important part of the sacrifice for the remission of sin. It is the blood of Jesus which cleanses us from all our sin. John tells us that blood and water flowed out from the side of Jesus. This could represent both communion (blood) and baptism (water). Both can represent a number of things. Ephesians 1:7 tells us, 'In whom we have redemption *through his blood*…..(italics mine)'. In Matthew 26:28 Jesus says, 'this is my blood of the new testament, which is shed for many for the remission of sins.' In 1 John 5:6-8 we read about the threefold witness of the spirit, the water and the blood. The water and blood are also a witness to the fact that Jesus actually died. Medical doctors know that the presence of both in this way mean that the heart has failed and the patient has died. A living body produces blood, but a dead body produces a mixture of blood and water.

John was a key witness to the death of Jesus. He says, 'He knows that he tells the truth, and he testifies so that you also may believe.' The soldiers were witnesses that Jesus had definitely died. They would certainly have broken His legs had there been any doubt. Joseph of Arimathea and Nicodemus were also witnesses that Jesus had died, as they took His body away for burial. There would also have been others there who are not named, and had there been any doubt at all someone would certainly have said so.

John records three witnesses to the empty tomb. Mary, Peter and 'the other disciple' by which it seems he means himself. God knew the rumours and stories that men would try and circulate about the resurrection of Jesus, and so here we have the detail about the grave clothes recorded for us. It is clear that Jesus rose and the grave clothes were left just as there were. The burial wrappings were not torn off or disturbed in any way. Jesus had simply risen from them and they had collapsed just where they were. We have a wonderfully clear account here, including so many details of the death and resurrection of Jesus, that it makes any attempt to deny this simply ludicrous.

Study 10 – Chapters 20 & 21
Jesus' resurrection

Discuss/think about

If someone lets you down, do you find it difficult to forgive them? Do you then find it difficult to trust them again? How do you feel if you are not able to keep a promise, or if you betray a friend in some way? How do you try and put things right?

Read John 20:10-30 and 21:1-25

1. Why is it surprising that the first person to see Jesus, when He had risen from the dead, was a woman?

2. In previous chapters Jesus has often referred to the Father as 'my Father' and 'the Father'. What is significant about the way Jesus now refers to the Father in 20:17? Why is this significant?

3. Why has the writer of this Gospel made sure that the conversation between Thomas and Jesus is recorded? What is significant about the way Thomas addresses Jesus in verse 28 (20:28)?

4. Why was the Gospel of John written? (20:31 may help.) Having studied this book of John do you believe that Jesus is the Christ, the Son of God? And do you feel you have life 'in his name'?

5. Why do you think the disciples went fishing (21:3)?

6. Why does Peter jump into the water to go to Jesus?

7. What lesson can we learn from the story of the empty fishing nets which are transformed into full ones?

8. Why does Jesus ask Peter three times about his love for Him?

9. What can we learn from this exchange between Peter and Jesus and the job that Peter is given?

10. What is the most significant thing you have learned from studying this Gospel of John?

Don't forget to pray

Ask God to fill you with His Holy Spirit so that you are able to put into practice all you have learned while studying the Gospel of John. Ask the Lord Jesus to help you understand what it means to have 'life in his name'.

John – Chapters 20 & 21
Study notes

The first person to see Jesus after He had risen from the dead was Mary. It is surprising and encouraging that such an important part was given to a woman at that time in history. We know that women were seen as unimportant in comparison to men and not given positions of prominence. If someone wanted to invent this story, at this point in time, then the last thing they would have done was to have given this part to a woman. Time after time God surprises us, and at the same time makes it clear that this is His word and absolutely true.

We can see that something has changed in the conversation between Jesus and Mary. Something is different because Mary did not, at first, recognise Him. She is told to tell the disciples that Jesus is going to, 'my Father and *your* Father, my God and *your* God.' This is the first time that He has referred to the Father in this way. But now, His work has been accomplished on the cross and the way has been opened for us to have a personal relationship with God through Jesus Christ. We can know God as *our* Father!

The conversation between Jesus and Thomas is a great encouragement to us, and the millions of those who have believed – *and not seen.* Thomas also says to Jesus, 'My Lord and my God!' He is the first person in this book to address Jesus as 'My God'. John has skilfully brought us back to the beginning of His book. 'In the beginning was the Word and the Word was with God and the Word was God.'

As we saw at the beginning of this study, John is writing because he wants us to be totally convinced that Jesus is the Son of God, God Himself come down to earth in human form. He wants us to understand that by believing in Him, our lives on earth will be changed and we will also find everlasting life. John wants us to know Jesus personally and find in Him water for this life, and also the water of everlasting life.

We don't really know why the disciples went fishing. Peter seemed to be very impetuous and perhaps after the tumult of all that had taken place he was trying to get things back to normal. In any case it is a very good lesson for us. If we go off and try and achieve things with our own ideas, and in our own strength, we will achieve nothing. But if we are going because Jesus has told us to go, then the nets will be full. If we have been working hard but seeming to achieve nothing, then perhaps we should pause and go to Jesus. Ask Him what we should be doing and where we should be doing it, so that He can fill our nets.

Peter leapt into the water when he realised Jesus was there, again acting impulsively. On the other hand, he clearly loved Jesus dearly and he had unfinished business with Him after having denied Him. Perhaps this was why he was in such a rush to reach Jesus. What grace and love Jesus shows by asking Peter three times about his love for Him. Peter denied Jesus three times. Now he has the chance to affirm his love for Jesus three times.

Most of us would not dream of giving such an important job to someone who had denied us in the way Peter denied Jesus. He is given the job of feeding the sheep and the lambs, i.e. the followers of Jesus. We also know from Matthew 16:18 that Jesus had told Peter that he was the rock on which the church would be built. It is clear from this exchange at the end of John that Jesus had not changed His mind because of Peter's denial. We have a wonderful God who is able to give us a second chance even when we mess up. R T Kendall has written a wonderful book which is recommended reading on this subject – 'Second Chance: Whatever Your Failing, God Can Use You Again.'

John makes it clear at the end of his book that he can only write down some of the things Jesus did. His objective has been to attract us to Jesus and to make it clear who He really is. God come down in human form, the light of the world, the resurrection and the life, the way, the truth and the life, a Saviour, Shepherd, Friend and much more besides. Do you know Him and do you have life in His name?

Other Books by Margaret Weston

Margaret Weston is the author of the BSBP series and the 'How do I know?' series.

'How do I know?' Series

The 'How do I know?' series consists of an ongoing conversation between two people. The first book **'How do I know I know God?'** would be invaluable for you if you claim to be a Christian but are not sure whether you do have a personal relationship with God. It would also be helpful for those who have no faith and yet are intrigued by those who do. It is a best-seller in Christian Evangelism.

One of the reviews on Amazon.com says this about the book. "Every question you've ever had about God is considered in the light of what the Bible says. If you count yourself as a skeptic, I think you'll find every argument you've ever had with God will be resolved in this book."

'How do I know what God wants me to do?' is the second book in the series and is written as a challenge to the author herself and to Christians world-wide. Will you realise your potential in Christ? Will you take action - or if you are already doing so, will you continue to take action - to advance God's kingdom in our generation?

The third book in the series is **'How do I know God answers prayer?'** which is a question every Christian should be able to answer! However, the book also looks at the subject of prayer in a wider sense as the two unknown people continue to discuss this subject together. You will find questions that are often asked by those who know God, and also those who do not.

BSBP Series

This series is intended to be for a specific group of people – those who really want to study the Bible but find they simply do not have the time. Life can be so hectic and whilst there are many very good Bible studies and commentaries available, these can be quite off-putting for very busy people.

The studies do not claim to be an in-depth look at a particular book of the Bible. They are meant to be used as an overview and to help the reader obtain a good grasp of the subject matter without having to use hours of their time.

At the date of publication of this study the following studies are available in the BSBP series:- John; Hebrews; Ruth and Esther; Job; 1 Corinthians; James; Revelation Part 1 and Revelation Part 2.

Full details of all the books in both the **'How do I know?'** and the **BSBP series** can be found on the following websites. The books are all available from Amazon and selected bookstores.

http://www.howdoiknowbooks.com

https://www.amazon.com/author/margaretweston

Printed in Great Britain
by Amazon

16328347R00041